The Ease of Forgetting

The Ease of Forgetting

HARNIDH KAUR

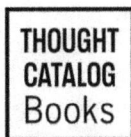

THOUGHT
CATALOG
Books

BROOKLYN, NY

THOUGHT CATALOG Books

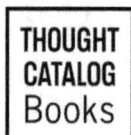

Published by Thought Catalog Books, a division of The Thought & Expression Co., Williamsburg, Brooklyn. Founded in 2010, Thought Catalog is a website and imprint dedicated to your ideas and stories. We publish fiction and non-fiction from emerging and established writers across all genres. For general information and submissions: manuscripts@thoughtcatalog.com.

First edition, 2017

ISBN 978-1945796333

Printed and bound in the United States.

10 9 8 7 6 5 4 3 2 1

To the reader

I hope you find grace in forgetting.

CONTENTS

Flying

Falling

The Carpenter

You make me feel like you
built the sun for me in your
little backyard shed, crouching
over incandescent bulbs as
you extracted light from them
and shaped it between your
fingers, cursing at the sizzles
and singes that burned welts
and callouses in your palms,
which you used to splatter white
against the shingled blue roof,
painting skies for me, giving
them texture and hiding my
name between the folds so that
I could find it and laugh—only
to have you keep a jar open to
collect my giggles, which you
filled into your pen, and wrote out
letters for me to read on my
saddest days, on paper you tore
off from the diaries of loneliness
that I kept, every loop of your
cursive a promise to never let
them be filled again, every full
stop a kiss of reassurance, and
you made paper boats out of
those letters, and let them out into
the wet alleys, holding my hand

as I tried to chase, lacing your
fingers through mine—a silent
oath of happier, lovely days.

Taxidermy

I want your heart, and I don't
mean that in a romantic way,
no, I mean it literally, for if I
was a criminal of the worst
kind, it's your heart I'd want to
smuggle out of your chest
to sell in the blackest of markets
because yours is the kind of
heart that would sell the best—
throbbing, and real, and vital,
it beats for more than just the
simple (well, not to me) purpose
of keeping you alive, it beats
for so much more, and that's
why, I have a vague inkling, that
even if I did manage to get my
hands on your heart, I wouldn't
be able to sell it, I'd rather have
the very core of you staring at
me through a jar of formaldehyde
kept right in front of me, on
my polished rosewood work desk.

Destination

If I were blind, and my only
sense that would let me see
the wonders of literature was
touch, I'd hunt you down in
Braille, and feel up and down
the body of your texts, absorbing
each simile, and metaphor, and
arbitrary alliteration, till I'd have
worn down the letters and absorbed
you into my fingertips, till my palms
smelled of you, and till I could
walk around with smears of ink
on my cheek, and I think you know
you'd be my favourite book, even
if I was told I wasn't meant to read it.

Linguistics

The Eskimos had (have?) a thousand
words for snow—each described a facet,
worshiped the source of their existence,
traced the histories of their interaction
with what fed, and killed them, they strung
them together til each sentence was a
prayer and the tongues caressing them were
just lapping at blessings till they melted
into each other, artist and muse fusing.

The Egyptians had (have?) fifty words
for sand—if murmured together they create
a cacophony that can be heard over the
storms that grace the most torrid desert
days, and some of the words, when repeated
like incantations, can bring forth an oasis,
and they taste like the dripping of plump
dates into parched mouths, like the first
sip of water touched cracked, swollen lips.

I had (have?) more words at my disposal
than I should, for I have bitten into books
and devoured them whole, I have swallowed
legacies in one gulp and spluttered them out
in rejection, and yet, for you, I have none to
spare, all the words I carefully choose, seem
to evaporate under the mingled heat of bare
skin against skin, bare, and my silence is
all I can give, all I have, and all I can share.

Fission

Falling in love feels like expanding—

suddenly, you're growing, billowing
out of your skin, and your skin is
the sky, each story you tried to bury
so deep fluttering like kites as they
skitter across your cheeks, resting
in the hollow if your temples, trickling
till they're tracing a map down your
face, welcoming kisses like check
points, each saving a little cache
of feelings at every stop they take.

suddenly, you're the universe, and
you grow constantly, swallowing up
worlds in the words you steep in the
water you find yourself thirsting for
on the most terrible summer days,
you are the hunger in pit of an empty
belly, but you are nourishment too—
gulping down yourself time and time
again, discovering new tastes, smells,
meats that have to be cut against grain.

suddenly, your lungs have grown and
you're breathing in ways you didn't know
your body could; you find a spot right
under your diaphragm, dusty, hollow,
forgotten, where air never reached and

you never knew it was meant to, and
you gulp in sweetness that breaks you
into half, only to reassemble you with
sparkly cogs and a hidden bit of magic.

suddenly, all the secrets you had hidden
in the spaces between your bones, written
on thin paper and stuffed through your
nose in the dead of the night, come spilling
forth, and the bleed through the cracks in
your skin, till your raw flesh welcomes the
seeds of wildflowers that bloom till their
roots writhe themselves through your veins
and into the ground, where you are now
embedded—and happier, kinder for it.

suddenly, you know you're in love, like
you had always wanted to be.
it's nothing like what you had thought.

Three Things

for s&a

i. it's okay to be kind when
the world demands of you
harshness—it's okay to be
soft, worn cotton in a room
full of starched, pleated
edges that poke into warm
flesh—it's okay to be home.

ii. it's okay to love, and be
proud of it, carrying it like
a clarion call that cuts into
a haze of people trying so
hard to unlearn words of
unmitigated, relentless joy
—it's okay to be satisfied.

iii. it's okay to look for
ferocious joy when you're
told to limit your heart to
lukewarm care, measured
desires, and inoffensive
increments of affection—
it's okay to hope recklessly.

Morse

Close your eyes and turn to
me, and let me transfer all
the memories we made to
you—lips pressed to your
earlobe as I use vibrations
and reminisces to paint
elaborate pictures in the
hues of the the end of
summer, dappled yellow and
spotted brown, their
monotony broken by the
sudden carmine of the
bougainvillea that survived
the culling of the seasons,
holding on to the thorns
as they poked holes through
the paper skin, letting
pinpricks of muggy sunlight
in, punctuated by the pungent
whiffs of the beginnings of
rot, underlined by the wafts
of sultry human smells; crushed
against each other, bodies
writhing like the urge to leave
against barricades rising to
keep them in. I always hated
the summer, hated the heat,
but your hands were always

cold, and so I gave you summer
as I saw it, felt it, and lived it,
incriminations of the schism
that bound us, contradictions.

Definitions

I like the idea of being home
not a shelter, but home,
for shelters are temporary, and
meant to be left for safer ones,
and they are uncertain, for
they could collapse
at the sight of a harsher storm,
no, i like the idea of being home.
Because you move shelter to
shelter, till you can't anymore
and you know, that broken,
beaten, and bruised, irrespective
of the harms you've done, and
those you've received like lashes
on your very being, you can limp
back home, and find solace, and
comfort, and healing, because
home is where you run to, not
run away, scared, from.

Creaking

At the hint of your arrival, I moved
again after years of waiting, and waited
I had, I was finally pushed to care about
a new advent, and I did—the tresses of
my hair rippled down my back, shaded
fountains gurgling like newborns choking
on their mothers' breast, and the limbs,
usually splayed in casual disarray, were
constructed into airy rooms, each of
them, overlooking the undulating expanse
of my skin, which was traversed over
by adventurous fingers, that probed their fill,
feeling lush murmurs grow on what had
been abandoned as an expanse barren
of all wants that seemed to have been
castoff, past being fulfilled, and slowly,
my shape emerged, pipes and stairs creaking
for I was a home now, one built for you
to find solace in, and as everyone waits
for you to step and stake claim, I smile
softly, knowing your moves before you do,
you never knew homes, and my being
one made especially for you, has not
changed what we've always considered true.

Literary Devices

I see poetry in everything now,
and I can't stop (I tried), I can't
not see metaphors in you, or
similes in the way you smile,
I tried to stop filtering the sound
of your footsteps into an onomatopoeic
device, I forced myself to ignore
your gait, which my heart wanted
to personify, I felt my hands
tremble, aching to reach out,
to wrap themselves around
an ink pen, to write you down in
the most obscure lines I can,
a code only you and I understand,
and it scares me to know my
whispers to you will never just
be just those—they will always
be incantations, mumbled spells
hoping to break you down into
cozy alphabets and comfortable
letters—that's all I can fathom,
that's all I've ever known, and
your strangeness makes me
tremble in my very bones.

Revelation

I know a lot of words, and I know
the synonyms to just as many,
and I've spent my life reading,
trying to contextualise what I do,
and when I try to write, I reach for
the thesaurus—words piled upon
words piled upon words piled upon
words, syllable after syllable, after
syllable, consonants crashing in my
mouth like cymbals thrashed against
without any meter or tone, all just
mere squiggles on paper that forced
me to imagine worlds I couldn't ever
comprehend, and in this cacophony
of letters and spellings, I chanced upon
a book that sat with me patiently,
unravelling the tightly wound litany of
words I knew, but never understood,
and now that I think about it, falling in
love is a lot like finally looking up the
meaning of a word you've used,
uncomprehendingly, all your life.

Mayer

I never quite bothered with instruments,
but I always thought I'd look good
with a guitar in my hand, so I read
about how one works,
I read till I could curl my fingers
into the air,
and pluck at strings that weren't there,
and I did this every night till I met you,
and suddenly,
my fret board was your back,
each vertebrae grooved against my fingertips,
leaving callouses on my hands,
I could make you gasp out
rickety notes as I plucked
my way down your chest and bones,
and I splayed my hand against the hollow of your neck,
holding on, as the sway made me arch my back,
and that's when I knew why musicians on the stage
looked the way they tended to.

Sunshine

Cotton candy dripping down
my fingertips frosted with
periwinkle popsicles that claim
to taste of the sky, salted with
the sweat left on my lips
that marks the back of my
hands as I brush my damp hair
off my neck, leaving it bare
for your lips to trail, bitter and
sweet, sugar and spice,
summer tastes of dark desires
and twisted, lingering delights.

Persephone

The idea of hell has always
given rise to images of misery
and despair, and to the idea
of a master who wears a crown
of twisted horns, and speaks
with a forked tongue, bartering
souls and silvered promises
but sin, to me, is seduction
and honeyed words of beauty
that slither up my throat, and
out of my lips, to flow down
yours, and it's marks of love
that we leave on each other
hidden under veneers of guarded
civility, and sin is the look we
share across the table at a bar
when we're out with friends, and
we smirk at each other, because
if sin led to hell, it's the only place
we'd travel to, again and again.

Semicolon

I remember seeing a book in
the library, and wondering what
it said, but people kept checking
it out before i could, and that
left me rather grumpy and gray
so i decided to bide my time
and i waited, patiently, at the fray
adding my name to the list of
people who were in line to get
a copy of this elusive, mysterious text
finally, after days of pacing, and
planning that it took, i got my hands
on it, and smiled, because finally,
it was mine to read and look into, but
just as i was enthralled, the month
decided to end, and the library called
back, asking me to return what was
suddenly my favourite book, and i
sighed, annoyed, because i was just
about to reach the end, and handed it
back, waiting again, to get my hands
on it, with restless, baited breaths.

Momentary

The sky and earth meet
but they do so only once
and that's when the eye
chances upon a horizon,
but as any student of
physics would tell you,
his voice coated with
derision, the earth never
truly meets the sky, it's
just a trick of light, one
that's cruel, on some days,
and it ends with the night.

Mappa Mundi

Mapping places needs cartographers,
and not just ones made to traverse,
it requires someone who wishes to
unfurl all the secrets hidden in the
crevices of the lands that he's
meant to discover, and if I was a piece
of land, I'd be one with a topography that
befuddles, for it moves from flat plains
to slopes, and hills that roll down into
lakes that pool only when incited to, and
if lands had choices, they'd choose the
explorers they wish to see unravelling
secrets, carefully, and if I was asked for
a name, whose fingers I wanted to feel
tracing me, I think you know that it's
you I would name for all to see.

Ripening

Tell me you see the way sunlight
cuts across my face, shadows and
skin kissing down my jaw, spring
dripping off my chin, hints of winter
caressing my neck, hidden in the
wave of hair crashing against my
nape—tell me you see me the way
I think you do, and warm the halves
of me still cold; fill them up with drops
of an elusive, unremembered summer
I unlearned, and can't find anymore.

Tumbling

I fell from grace some time ago
and found myself in wonderland
where i met people of my kind
and drowned myself in worship
of hedonism, and lust, and reckless
abandon, and i saw my body change
from rigid certainty to languid chance
and the liquor flowed with distinct
disregard, and we drank it down with
forbidden fruits from the garden
that only grew the ripest jewels, and
no one was thrown out for dissent,
and the voices were never drowned
out by righteous protest, and the acceptance
i found made me question my fall,
for was it from grace, or into it?

Tremors

My hands shake when I write
but only when I do so with a
particular brand of pens that
I seem to buy every time I go
to the shop, and I never know
why, and how, I land up with
a box of them in my desk, and
I'm telling you this because of
all the people I know, and all
the stories I've read, and all the
music I've heard, you're the only
person who knows what it's like
to stare at a white blank page
when the cave drags you back
into it, on the most unexpected days.

Battlegrounds

Armed with stories, you and me
our interactions are a battlefield
of who has more notches on the
barrel of the guns we carry, each
bullet unfurling into smoke and
haze, every command laced with
metaphors of pain, and loss, and
longings, and each retreat is a
testament to the beauty we can
create, and for all the love between
us, we're storytellers and weavers
of tales, and the wounds we leave
are so well hidden under vagaries
of alliterative assaults, that we leave
absolutely no trace of our guilt.

Palette

I have too many colours
splashed on too much
skin, and it floats far too

freely, with no anchoring
of darker hues and softer
charcoal lines, no shadows

to underscore and highlight,
no depth, no width, no grain

come

soak into me, swirl through
the chaos, cut through the
cacophony, stalk the dripping
canopies of scattered dreams

underline me.

Policy Solutions

Let's just ban marriage and love
and affection on the streets, and
make it a crime to land a peck on
someone's cheek, and attach looks
of alarm and disgust to anyone
who claims to be helplessly crushed
by infatuation and everyone who
writes sonnets about adoration in
passing phases, for maybe when
all loves are illegal, and all crushes
are crushed with an intent of a
crime, love affairs will make hardened
criminals out of us, and of course,
nothing spells romance like hidden
rendezvous, some mystery, and
whispered meetings, clandestine.

Klutz

I'm clumsy with technology and emotions

and you knew that right from the start
when you saw me fumble thrice with
the lock screen on my phone, my stubby
fingers drawing it wrong, and you pried
it from my hand, and calmed my shaking
digits down, tapping the screen for me
so that I could make the call, and you
did much the same with your heart,
clasping your fingers over mine, and them
over your throbbing core, and when I
dropped my phone the umpteenth time,
or left scratches on your soul, you just
smiled, and picked them both up, for

I'm clumsy with technology and emotions
and you knew that right from the start
but I don't know how long that knowledge
alone will keep you from replacing me
as the keeper of your bruised heart.

Dilli

We sit across each other, your hand on mine,
fingers caressing palms, reading a story to which
tracings upon tracings led, absent minded face,
you asked me what I was dreaming of, I smiled,
and said, "You and Delhi.", much to your mild
bemusement, and you laughed a little, leaning in,
curiosity lighting up your eyes like India Gate at
7 p.m., your lips against my forehead, leaving wet
kisses shaped like CP's outer circle, each block
shaped like a bite mark, and your fingers dapple
my back like the sunlight streaming through the
trees near the ridge, your knees against mine,
crowded like Rajiv Chowk metro station at 11 a.m.,
and suddenly, I feel breathless, burying my face
into my hair, imagining the smell of rewaris and
popcorn that just wasn't there, and I shift away,
trying to arch into the absent cold in the air, feeling
the slight damp on my skin, aching for a Delhi
winter afternoon that I wish we could share.

Wavering

Tripping

I don't take the stairs anymore,
choosing, instead, to lumber up
ramps and elevators, and often
scampering up concrete slabs,
and when I do, when I must, I
cling on to the railing like my
knees are on the verge of giving
way—I walk like I'm absolutely
sure that my toes will somehow
entangle themselves into my
hair, and fall off, dangling in
my face as I lose balance and
trip down, head first, into a
fast approaching blackness;
I don't think I'm scared of
falling, no, I've bruised and
broken myself enough to know
that's not worth being scared of—
I think what I'm afraid of now
is the
fact
that
nobody
cares.

Flight Status: Unknown

Never pick up someone from
the airport, or drop them to one-
airports are the gateways
to the beginnings and middling
grounds, but they never signify
the end, or that's what I always
thought, till I paced at an airport
waiting for someone to land safe
and sound, and to take him into
my arms, and till I dropped him
back to the airport, and felt my heart
clench just a little bit into my ribs,
and that's why I'm going to try and
never pick up someone from
the airport, or drop them to one,
because my heart can run with
beginnings, and not shatter at
ends, but it doesn't cope quite
so well with the middling grounds.

Diagnosis

I wish I could reduce myself
down to just my nervous system,
a network of translucent, spidery
gossamer threads, bound into
a starfish's shape with a bundle
that runs down from my head
to tail, and i wish i could whittle
away all my skin and muscle and
sinew and flesh, till all i had left
was the cause of why i felt how
i did, and maybe when i was
nothing but neurotransmitters
and the crevices of my mind, and
the arch of my spine, is when i'll
be able to explain exactly why
and how and when i felt, with the
intensity of how i thought i did.

Urban Renewal

If I was a city, I'd be one marred by
civil strife, and men killing men in
the name of law, because they called
that very law out for its hypocrisy,
and if I were a city, I'd be one in the
news for rising crime rates, and eerie
abandoned boroughs, ones that the
disillusioned, semi-educated twenty-
somethings would desecrate further
just because they have nowhere else
to go, and I'd be a honeytrap they walked
so innocently into, and if I was a city,
my love, you'd be robbed, not of your
gold, but of your heart, because those
who walk in once, find it impossible to part.

Confession

Grade eight saw me struggle
with mathematics till I was
finally defeated, but arrogant,
as I was, I refused to ask any
questions in class, and when
my teacher realized I never
quite understood what she
taught, she asked me why I
didn't speak up, and I claimed
fear was my folly, though it
truly was not, all I was afraid
of, and still am, is the possibility
of me appearing daft, and I
think I never learned my lessons
(either in class, or life), for
asking the right questions would
ease my path, but for that, I'd
have to forgo my silly might.

Effort

Loving you was never
effortless
it was always the most
effortful
thing i did and i
did it with pride
because you deserved
all my nights and
you needed all my
days in a time
when all i had to give
was my tattered heart
which you claimed
with calloused hands
and battered arms
and bruised lips
that left a trail of
angry confessions
on my chest.

Schedule

My day is spread around me
like the falling of leaves in a
rainstorm—askew, lonely, with
an almost bereft air that shrouds

bits of me that make up the
space I take; vines creep out from
under my fingernails to curl
around empty patches of air

that slither down my lungs and
get stuck somewhere around my
third rib—suddenly I'm larger than
I thought I was and smaller than

what I could be, I'm floating in
a half grown state, my sleeves
too long but pant hems skimming
unwieldy calves that trip and

screech against each other on
empty roads that I skip on from
one puddle of light to another,
careful to not let my toes dip

into darkness (the monsters
there bite and burrow into my
skin without asking if I would
like to be a home for their nips)

and my day shrinks around me
wrapping tighter against my
body til it's cradling me against
itself, 'shh,' it says, 'we'll be home

soon, then you can spread your
weary wings' but by the time I
reach, I have forgotten how to
spread them, or that I have any.

Redefinition

You see, the first time we kissed,
I did not feel like I was coming home—
the jolts that ran down my spine were
unknown, the way your hands held
me, hard enough to mark, felt like
anger and passion and fear dancing
from the tip of your tongue to mine

You see, the first time we kissed,
home tore itself into little pieces of
confetti with razor edges that left a
hatched pattern down my face, and
as I dripped blood, you dipped your
fingers into it, smearing it around my
lips, calling me your own little storm.

You see, the first time we kissed,
you claimed you felt magic around us,
and sawing me in half was the greatest
trick you ever did, leaving me crushed
from the bottom of my lungs to the top
of my thighs, hollow space where you
let your darkness coil and slither.

You see, the first time we kissed,
should have been the last, because
every hair on the nape of my neck stood
up like an exclamation mark, warning
me to stay away, and I confused the

forest fire burning through you with
the warm hearth I had yearned for.

Un-

Don't use the word 'home' anymore—

call it a promise not kept, a kiss unkissed,
a call not made, a letter not sent, a giggle
left ungiggled, a meal not cooked, a cooked
one not fed, a book read halfway, a story
left unsaid.

call it a passport page bitten into, a ragdoll
unheld, a house key unneeded, a house that
does not exist, a lane left uninhabited, a cup
left unfilled, a heart unbeating, a long life
left unlived

don't call it home

home is where the 'un's don't exist.

Kaleidoscope

I could use your eyes to
show you a world within
the world that you know,
hold your eyelids open by
the tips of your eyelashes,
just hard enough to force
sight to flood your mind,
where I could build castles
out of the sand I pour into
your ears, watching it rise
grain by grain, shaping it
into fantastic turrets and
moats deeper than you
ever thought your own
mind could ever find
itself swimming, with the
anglerfish of your psyche
nodding their hesitant hellos,
and I could make you see
what I wish for you, with
the same effort it would
require for me to breathe;
but tonight, I'm going to
sit by, and wait for you, and
hold my tongue as I do,
I'm a storyteller, and I've
always been, but tonight I
need a story to put me to sleep.

Thrumming

Mornings start with the shuffle
of feet against the tiled floor,
whisper of cheap, fake georgette
rubbing against itself, static, buzz,
never reaching electric fulfillment,
the clip of a ceramic mug against
the edge of the glass top, making
the wood of the table grunt against
that of the bed, angry, stubborn inertia,
the muddled crackle of the newspaper
damp with the heavy water-bearing air,
interspersed with the muffled clap and
clomp of utensils being shifted, lids
clanging like the cymbals stirring out
of control from a young drummer's hands—
quiet whirrs of the refrigerator now
punctuates the shrill screech of the
food processor, rising up in crescendo
with the sizzle pop crackle of a single egg
(fried with a little shimmer of pepper
glinting off the white, black granules
wading through yellow glimmer grease),
paired with the stunned alarm of the
toaster letting off its ward, unharmed
except for the slight char echoing the
metallic bands of orange heat branding
through the carefully timed traps—

stillness is a lost language in a world
defined by violent sounds and smells.

Unintended

I am a mistress of the words
and a witchling who bewitches
letters and sentences into webs
that enchant and beguile all who
enter the world of images and
wonders I create, and one thing
I've always been irrationally proud
of is the fact that I'm never found
speechless, or for want of ways
to express what I feel, and yet
today, I'm left without any way to
show you what I need you to see
and when I laughed about wanting
to be left breathless by someone,
I didn't mean for this to ever be.

Neuroscience

I used to smoke, and a lot, at that,
and I quit it, cold turkey one day—

it wasn't easy, my nose still traces
the traces of nicotine that stain the
air like they once stained my teeth,

but I'm okay now, I suppose, I have
a list of vices that are presumably
under my control, and I count love

amongst that them, or I would, if
it actually were, but let me tell you
how love is manufactured (not by

capitalism, no, though that would
be a fine guess). There's a certain,
remarkable maliciousness to love,

the neuroscience behind it, very
telling of how, despite all that talk
of being the most powerful predators,

we're still prey to the fallacies
of fancy and words. The amygdala is
almond shaped, sitting pretty like

the crown jewel on the temporal
lobe, near the side of your head—you
wouldn't notice it, unless you paid

careful attention (just like she would
have slipped away if you didn't catch
the sparkle of her ring against the

bar's strategic dim lighting), and its
size belies the histories of its growth
(just like how you would've never

guessed how a body that tiny could
hold so much anger, and beauty, and
passion), and this is where the neurons

that engage the stress response in
your body fire from (like the sparkling,
venomous barbs she shot at you,

leaving physical reactions in their
wake), leading to a fight or flight
syndrome (you barricading yourself

into the bathroom for three hours,
making mental lists of the
pros and cons of leaving at that very

moment), now mixed with all the
serotonin your brain could produce,
and then some more (your lips against

her neck as you felt the thrum of her
heartbeat pick up with yours), and
you fought, you fought, you fought,

first her, then the doubts, then yourself—
always finding reasons to make up
and make pretty till you found an

unknown reflection on the mirror

you never knew you had on the roof—
　　if you were to be diagnosed, it

　　would have been with addiction,
　　not love, not romance, not want,
　　not need, just sordid inability.

(but you already knew that, didn't you?)

Crystallization

Do you remember the English
grammar exercise we did in
grade school, where you were
given an answer, and had to
decipher what the question
could be? I was given a
similar exercise in college
today, and our professor
said, with a little smile on her
face, "you know the syllabus,
and you have the answer
prepared, why don't you try
to structure the question
you have an answer to, to
make it seem like the perfect
fit?" so I sat and contemplated,
nearly ten years after the
first time I did this, and I
realised that finding the correct
questions to ask, is almost,
if not more difficult, than
riddling what the answer is.

Plunder

Bombay is made up of seven islands-
seven independent bodies of land,
bound together with history of
angry, violent consolidations, stolen
from sea, given to man, nestling on
narrow strips of land; the crush
of dreams that threatens to choke,
as one after another, they topped off
the tapering edges of the shores,
eager to join the sea as it wrecks
havoc on the three-legged stones
meant to keep it away, always the
unapproachable mirage of expected
returns and gains, and I lay curled
next to you, your body shore, sea, land,
sins, each square inch of you trampled upon by
the force of the imaginations I've foisted
on your shoulders, wreathed with strands
of seaweed from the times you dragged me
back, fingers laced into my hair, from the sea
I kept trying to step back into, and you curl
around me, warm, dry, safe, and I wonder
if cities like me, hardened and held with steel
and concrete and rails, were truly ever homes
to people who still dreamed beyond themselves.

Drowning

Hold me down in water,
just six inches is enough to drag
me away, but you knew that since
the moment you pressed your palm
against the curve of my neck and pushed
down, carefully, with deliberation, and
held me with your fingertips, just so afraid
of water splashing back at you in the
off chance that I struggled against
the force of my lungs trying to heave
me upwards, arching, trying to sluice
through the rushing gray, but I don't,
I don't fight away, I stay, stay under
your palm, feeling water rip through
my nose and into the alveoli,
unequipped to handle the deluge, just
like I am unequipped to handle your
ministrations, and suddenly, the
pressure is gone, and I gasp up,
sputtering, coughing, sucking in air
like a greedy glutton, and as you peer
down at me, the cuffs of your shirt wet, I
say sorry, for the unfortunate inconvenience.

Schadenfreude

My favourite vice coats my tongue
in caramel caresses and bitter bites,
it's not an easy one to confess, for
it underlines my basest desires, it's
a representation of my hypocrisy, of
the fact that for all my benevolence
there's a part of me that cheers a little
when someone else spectacularly fails,
and I'd like to say I want to improve,
but I always liked my indulgences
bittersweet and shaded gray.

Bard

I have noticed that my cheeks
tend to be bitten raw by me
whenever I lie, a method of coping
with the anxiety that accompanied
the stress of creating, and holding
on, to the stories and their
chronologies—I have lied all my life,
and I have lived those lies, but
they're still an unfamiliar, and strange
terrain I trip and fumble with—
and the last time I spoke of love,
I read out something I'd written,
a delicate ditty on true love,
and I realised that the insides of my
cheeks weren't flesh anymore, they
were reddish pulp, chewed through,
ground out by molars unable to resist
biting the lies that flowed through.

The Biography of a Bullet

A bullet doesn't sound like you'd think,
it's not a clean snick against the sky,
or the crack of a narrow whip,
no, a gunshot sounds like incomprehensible
angerfearpainsadnesshurtaches,
a gunshot sounds like the violence
that echoes in its creation
a bullet shimmers in the air, wavering,
copper against blue, moving so fast it's
almost quite still, a bullet is hot
hotter than you'd think; boiling with
the rage of intent and destruction
but if you hear them often enough,
and if you get past them being just
gunshots, they sound like the drip
of a raindrop on a corrugated
steel roof, tinny and hollow, and
echoing with the promise of
instability, and today feels like
the stormiest night in a long time,
and every one of us is drenched.

Thermostats

I wake up at 2 a.m., sheets sticking
to my sides, sweat sliding down my
skin in rivulets, pooling in shallow
pools between the waves that make
up the curves of me, and I tear them
off with a tired hand, letting the fan's
creaking caress my back, slow, heavy
air, heavier than my sighs, kneading
at my flesh with unwieldy, uneven
fingers, cooling me down till I can
breathe again, and I stay like that, the
pillow turned over to the cooler side,
pressed against my cheek, taking up
only a fraction of the giant bed, the
fact that my arms can splay without
barriers, which is a sign of how,
despite the heat, without you lying
next to me, cold, I truly am.

Overlaps

I know the difference between
lonely, and alone, both semantic
and otherwise, and I know why
and how they're not interchangeable,
and I know how one's the feeling
of being alone, while the other is
simply the physical sense of the
same, and I know I shouldn't feel
lonely when I'm simply alone, with
myself, but knowing all this, and so
much more doesn't change the fact
that I'm alone, lying in my tiny bed,
and loneliness is my only friend.

Expulsions

I tend to fall out of love very neatly

I wrap my emotions up in the worn
bubble wrap they have barely emerged
from, the creases folding around the
edges like they never quite had enough
time to ease and fade away. My voice
fades back to words on paper, the lilts
and waves disappearing, absorbed
back into the ink, and that ink gets
darker again, finding itself whole
after years of lighter, brighter shades.

My body suddenly feels smaller, as
I let go of the universe I had allowed
into myself, and my lungs shrink, air
finding itself knocked out for the lack
of space. My hands, however, feel like
they have grown overnight, fingers
clumsier than before, joints heavier
than some time ago, and nails that
drag along surfaces trying to find
corners and crevices to hold on to.

Bottles of promises that still flicker
dimly are placed back on dusty shelves
where they rattle, struggling against
their eventual fade. Little ceramic boxes
of dreams are muffled by a blanket of

silence before they are hammered at
by unfamiliar realities, the crushed
pieces swept away carefully, not a
single shard left to cut into careless,
bare feet learning to dance again.

I tend to fall out of love very neatly,
neat enough to question if I ever
fell in love in the ways I thought I had.

Exorcisms

I could start fires with what I
feel for you, and I could burn
down houses if it meant I found
a home in what we were, but
now the flames are licking my
insides, and I'm letting them
consume me, slowly sapping
on all my vitality, because they're
flames that refuse to die until
they've burnt the description of
your face from the tips of my
fingers, which could trace it in
the empty air, and all I can do
is sit, staring at my hands, and
beg them to stop imagining that
you're next to me, with me, here.

How to Apologise to your Lover

i. hold her like she's your only
truth, and you, her only witness,
validate her being with proofs
of worth, of want, of faith

ii. bow down in front of her,
kneel with your head bowed, and
let her fingers lace through your
hair, do not move under her gaze

iii. let her take control, cease all
resistance, do not wince when
she tugs at you, anger, pain, ache
flowing through her tips to your roots

iv. when you're on the verge of
screaming out loud, scream her name
instead, scream it till you forget
yours, each breath stained with her

v. dissolve yourself into a cup of tea
with just enough sugar to cut through
your sour, hope that she will sip on
curdled, ruined milk in any case.

Expiration Notice

I am not afraid of running out
of words to give, I know, I will
some day, for mine belong to
the world, and are cripplingly
limited—

no, what I fear is a
little worse, a smidgen darker,
a trifle quieter—

what I fear in
my loneliest moments is

not
having any silences to share,

no
glances to exchange,

no
touches to convey,

no
kisses
to pray on someone else's
chest,

no
comfort given with bodies
and hands,

no
negative spaces to highlight
the muddy glory

of bright colours
and brighter days.

The Readers

You say we're not on the
same page, and that we
might have to slam the
book shut, but what if we
are, but on different lines,
and reading the points of
view of characters stuck
in melancholic strife, and
all we need is to close our
eyes, and readjust, and
realign, start this paragraph
again, maybe take into
cognizance the metaphors
and the line breaks, for I
don't know about you, love,
but once I put a book down,
I find it extremely hard to
pick up and start all over again.

Hyphenated

Shame on you for changing,
and shame on me for staying
just where you left me, solid
in a flux of fluid realities, each
wave rooting me deeper into
the sand—funny, how easy it
is to brush off when dry, and
how it clings to me, like water
does to it, fixing me into place
and sucking me into shapes
that make no more sense, since
the day you changed, and i was
lost, only fitting in your context.

Fire Escape

I remember asking you once
why I never saw pictures of
you together, and you smiled
a brittle little smile, and said
that you deleted them all off
every account you had, and
she didn't need to, because
she never put any up, it was
always you who showed open
affection, and it was you who
loved the most, and when it
was time to leave, her bags
didn't have to be packed, because
she never unpacked hers, and
I smiled back a smile just as
brittle, because as you said that
out loud, I realised that you
hadn't ever put a picture of us up.

Architecture

Your body is a house, the only
one you have, and your mind
allows you to decorate each part
of it like you wish, it lets you try
to create a home out of every
room in it, and the way you live
is chosen by design, one that
you create, and you could live in
the opulence of arrogance, or the
cozy comfort of love, within the
sleek lines of constructed pride, or
the open meadows of ambitious
worlds, or you could live in fear,
and sadness, and anger, each one
bearing down on you like walls
closing in, around your very soul
and being, and the walls are dank,
drab, and peeling, and it's terrifying
to try and leave when it's all you
know, but when you've worked so
hard till now, you deserve a better,
bigger, beautiful hearth and home.

Flying

Dear Fourteen-Year-Old Me,

I don't have much time, the flux capacitor
is charging, so here are seven things I think
you should know, seven truths I wish I was
told, seven lessons I wish I was taught, just
seven anchors to pull me to safe shores.

i. you'll be glad to know how far we've come
in our nail color choices—from bitter black to
sparkly blue, from shades of anger to happier
hues.

ii. you'll be happy to know that the body we
own is safer now, and healthier too—we made
out alive from the pain, it's over now, it's home
again.

iii. love didn't forsake us the first time, it just
left for a little while, we're loved in so many
ways, it's astonishing on our most dreary
days.

iv. on days when we're stripped off our words,
of the worlds that we can build and burn, all
we have is our self, it's never too much, nor too
less.

v. we've not earned our keep till now, and that's
okay, for we've earned in laughter lines, and
frowns that spread, tapestries of the lives we've
lived.

vi. our love for letters has not dimmed, and we
get some in return for ones we write, and though
the sentences are half forgotten, they shine true and
bright.

vii. despite it all, through it too, we found reason
to live every day we wake up, anew—
if that's the only mark we leave, it's beautiful, and
worthy too.

Spring Cleaning

Think of yourself as a home—

slowly wipe away a year's worth
of grime from your heart, taste
the mistakes you made, bite off
their shells and suck on the lessons
hiding under layers of regrets—

place little lamps down your
spine and arch back till the oil
spills down your skin, use the
singe marks as a map to find
your way back to yourself—

paint your skin with colours
that stand out, stark against
your knuckles and nails, write
words of kindness, love, joy
read them till you can't forget—

string rice lights down your
limbs, drape them around
your shoulders, till you drip
of honeyed drops of sunlight
caught between your lips—

throw your doors wide open,
smile a welcome to another
year of being, find yourself

curling up into a question
mark at night as you sleep.

Unclenching

Stop trying to hoard the forest
for a little while—stop clinging
on to that which wishes to not
stay
instead, with slow, steady
deliberation, choose one tree,
just the one in front of you,
walk
to it with palms outstretched,
welcome and surrender held up
in each hand; wait for the bark to
reach
for you with its cool tendrils,
offer up your eyes in exchange
of slow, steady memories collected
over
years of stillness, feel the blood
coursing through leaves as water
courses through your limbs, pluck
just
one bud, a new memory made
and carried away, held steady by
roots that knew the earth before it
was
yours.

Hope

There is a certain audacious challenge
to hope now—it doesn't end with a full
stop anymore, the punctuations have
shifted, and now it's followed by a soft,
hesitant pause before it settles on one—

hope?
questions a pair of tired eyes far away
from home, dragged through dust and
heat as the anger boils over, sweeping
away.

hope!
exclaim a pair of hands that have worked
tirelessly, day and night, to build a fire that
warms aching palms, scar tissue overwriting
fate.

hope,
explains a hesitant voice, careful to add a
justification, a clarification for its ability,
it's privilege to continue searching for better
days.

hope.
stands waiting, arms outstretched, arching
out to embrace those who cling on to her
skin despite the buffeting waves of terrifying
hopelessness.

Three Things You Need to Know Today

i. your name is not supposed to be
easy, it is not supposed to be twisted
into mangled forms for tongues that
can't swirl and flick at your histories
and curves, your name carries power,
and the power is your worth—do not
let it be lessened for someone's comfort.

ii. you've come so far than where you were
exactly a year ago, if it was better than it is now,
at least you know that happier days can be
found, and you know that seasons fade in and
out—after every sapping summer, winter will
commence, it will flow down your withered
bones, and cool their feverish tempests.

iii. your body cannot help being what it
is, it cannot help being less than your
wants, more than your fickle demands,
hating it is easy, but loving it needs a
courageous heart—it's admitting that
love can heal, it's realising that forgiveness
is real, it's knowing your worth is
more than the accumulation of your parts.

Cardiography

you asked me what my heart is
made of—it cannot be flesh and
blood, you said, it is too strange,
too big, too small, too hard, too
soft, so I slipped my hand into
my chest, fingers through ribs,
and nails through muscle and
groped blindly into the pulpy
mess inside, only to find what
looked like an almost-dimmed
firefly—the kind with tails that
shine not-bright, legs that bend
in ways not-fine, bodies crumpled
from being clutched at and kept
in jars not-big, wings that have
creased into themselves, origami
imitations of what was once real,
solid, and not-chimeric, quivering
as it shines against time—still real,
still shining, still beating, still alive.

Orchard

Winter has gone, and summer
slowly creeps, breathing is heavy,
slow, quiet, clogged with salt and
water, laced with the scales of
fish I've never seen, and yet, when
I reach out to touch your skin I feel
Spring spring up as it pours down
my throat like a single sip of cool
water, marking its way down to my
stomach, and I'm suddenly made
of the palest pink gossamer, and
you're the sepals curled around me,
unfurling my limbs, and watching
as I drop inhibitions like pollen
that spreads its yellow seed on
loamy streets, and I find myself
sprouting, growing as I feed off
the way you watch me bloom, and
the soon, the merest echo of retracting
winter winds gasping goodbye, is all
that's left of all I've ever been.

The Doctor

I am sick, and recovering,
slowly, piece by piece,
gathering the petals strewn
at my feet; they bunch
together in my hand, crumpled,
staining my fingertips with
madness and the remnants
of quiet breaths, I tie them
up with black thread, holding
them together, a mockery
of my own—necromancy was
never the art I wanted
to be known for.

Escape Route

Before you ask me to leave,
I need you to return some things
I left with you for safekeeping, I
don't want this any more than you,
and I would like this to be a civilised
goodbye, so just give me back the
hours I put in, staying up with you
as you chased sunsets that were
never yours to begin with, and refund
those inches, metres, miles I travelled
to make sure you didn't fall asleep
without knowing how much you meant
to me, and while you're at it, try to
pick up the little notebook on your
bedside, the one I scribbled poems
out for you in, and you'll find an eraser
underneath—I wrote you out in pencils,
because to put your flaws down in ink
felt like a crime against what I felt,
but now that I look back, it was only
because I was building an escape route
for myself, a little exit to crawl through,
because you were a fire hazard waiting
to combust, and I guess what I'm saying
is that I don't want anything back from
you, because all I gave was of my own will,
but I refuse to give any more, I have
nothing left to fuel the fire you've built.

Reframing

I'm not a phrase, or a
cliché, or a gerund you
can tack on, I'm not the
past tense, nor the
idiom you chose instead,
nor am I a filler you
use, to fill the blank space
that you know naught of,
I'm whole, and I'm complete,
and I'm enough, and if I
was ever written down, I'd
be a singular sentence that
people would love to quote.

Benedictions

I hope you don't live in happy times—
they are linear, and boring, often
easily broken; may unhappy times
never mar your unmarked brow,
they break your heart and leave
you incapable of the smaller joys,
but if I had to wish you well, not
too much but just as long as you
stay away from hell, I'd wish for
you to live in days that sometimes
spell out 'riveting' for you, just
as often as you feel blue—may you
never have a boring day to your
name, may every moment spell
unending bedlam whispered in
the softest waves, may you never
find yourself sitting, aimless,
without a care, may you always
know the cost of being, and the
weight of existence that you
invite—maybe this is less a wish,
and more a curse for you to live,
but I hope it well, and hope it hard—
may your world be interesting
from near, as well as afar.

Woman

She's hot when she's angry,
like a storm you must tame,
and she's a seductress when
she's shy, and it's your duty to
make her bloom like she's been
meant for it, and she's a vixen
when she's intelligent, her ability
is yours to challenge and obtain,
and she's a tease when she says
she doesn't know, and of course,
it's your job to go ahead and
'educate,' and she's a little
template for all your desires,
but a whore, a slut, and a bitch,
if she tries to express her own
refrains, and that's why, I guess
she was obviously asking for it.

Scalded

I remember laughing at
a friend of mine, who,
after a one night stand,
got a dolphin tattooed on
her ankle, exactly like
the one her 'soulmate' (her
words, not mine) apparently
had, and she came back
disgruntled and annoyed,
because he was a broke bum
from Ukraine whose tattoo
was meant to only stay as
long as he did in Goa, that
is to say, maybe fifteen days,
and I remember laughing
so hard that I burnt my nose
with all the hot coffee I
managed to snort, and now
that I look at the mess I've
made, I know exactly what
she probably would've felt.

Things You Could Be, If You Were a Sheet of Paper

i. a paper boat sinking up and down the
ways of the gutter streams, floating, if
briefly, powered by hopes and hushed
giggles of childish gambles with the sky.

ii. a diary page crumpled into a ball, hiding
within itself a universe held in the palm
of another, anger and helplessness pulsing
through trembling fingers spelling denial.

iii. a note smuggled from one end of a class
to another, spelling out anticipation and
cotton candy dreams of sticky sweaty summer
songs sung in quavering, unsteady voices.

iv. a book page ripped out and folded seven
times, creases so deep that they change the
way the words sound in your mind, held close
when air doesn't reach the pit of your belly.

v. a kite built in a third-grade crafts exercise,
held together with ice cream sticks and sweet
white glue, tied down by the need for a better
grade, and yet aching to soar up and fly.

Fragments

People break so softly, it
sounds like nothing at all,
you can't hear it, hearts
aren't made of crystal, they
have no freedom to stall,
eyes have no time to grieve,
tears only last for so long;
if you want to ever know
who's broken, look for the
little signs—look for shoulders
steeped too low, or held too
straight, look for hands with
ragged tips, or ones that gleam
with unchipped paint, look
for voices that quiver softly,
or the ones that captivate the
stage—I think what I'm trying
to say is, everyone's a little
cracked and crumpled, and
they carry on living, loving, and
fighting in their own wicked,
strange, complicated ways.

Facets

I am earth: roots have grown in me
and I have let them,
feeding an entire universe
with my muscle and bone.

I am water: I have nourished,
and I have killed, my depths
have been untouched
by the ravages of man—

I am infinite.

I am air: I am conduit to passion,
anger, rebellion; the screams of
revolution have been screamed
into my skin.

I am fire: I have consumed
and burnt away histories,
I have warmed the coldest hearths,
I have lit the darkest days.

My body is a country and I have
been plundered by war, each inch
of me fought over and pillaged to
feed the blindest egos.

Horrors are tattooed up my back,
each word inked onto me, raised,

like braille, and hands pawing to
interpret what my wounds bled.

I am a book only I own, my nails
have carved an intricate language
into my tongue, and through its
twisted curves—I emerge.

I emerge from shadows I have
been pushed into, from the grave
I was buried in, mud clinging to
my limbs, I emerge—a lotus.

I am a fallen goddess, wings chopped
off and trailing down my back, halo
askew, I am human—warm body,
warm heart, warm enough to burn.

Heat pours off my reflection, I stand
unfettered, loud, growing into
and out of myself, screaming out
a litany of injustices.

I am alive, I am real, I am bruised, and
limping, anger pulsing off me in thumping
waves, each stomp screaming
'I am, I am, I am, I am.'

Ages 6 and Up

You held me like you held
the puzzle you had as a six
year old child—first, you probed
my crooked corners, your
fingers painted with questions
that smeared my edges till
they melted and blurred into
limpid curves that held no
shape, the interrogatives you
used left my angularities and
facets molten and misshapen,
but you were always a distracted
child, always curious, but never
quiet, and you lost your pivot
suddenly, just like you found
it nestled in the box in which I
came, so you turned your wrists
the other way, flicking your
palms, till time did too, and I
found my pieces strewn, astray,
caged back in the now sodden
cardboard container you shoved
somewhere under your winter wear;
I quietly wait, unruffled, for
you to open my box again, faded
stickers peeling off to reveal
a game you half-remembered,
because one day you will chance

upon me, and one day we will
meet again, and I will recognize
you from the sound of your breath,
and I'll be a stranger to you, for
I'm still made of little pieces,
but I learned how to render
myself so very differently.

Icarus

'He loved the sun too much,' they say,
of Icarus' terrible, tragic fate, but
none of them ever seem to remember,
what killed him was his watery grave,
so maybe it wasn't the sun to blame,
but the sea that wanted him to stay,
and hence she wreathed with steady care
seaweed through his rippling hair,
and dragged him in, under her sway,
luring him with her dancing waves.

Paused

'Come to the sea,' he says, surrounded
by swirls of blue, turquoise, and green,
but I sit, still, eyes closed, trying to count
the grains of sand between my toes,
and he calls again, 'why won't you
come to me?' and I ignore him again,
pressing my palm down, watching my
fingers sink deeper into the dampness,
and he joins me, sitting knee to knee,
shoulder to shoulder, trying to lace
his fingers into mine, like has been
done, innumerable times. I pull away,
and dig my fingertips right back into
the sand—I need time to rebuild the fragile
castle the waves wash away, again and again.

Incantations

I'm not broken, even though
I may have cracks in my skin
that shine through, and when
they do, you see silver, gold
and amethyst sparkling in my
very veins, because I fix myself
again and again, simply because
I refuse to remain shattered, for
I owe it to myself, and to the
ones who love me, to respect
what has gone into creating me,
and it's not just blood, bones, sinew
and muscle, no, I'm made up of
starbursts, wild waves, storms,
hurricanes, and the oldest magic
that goes beyond what has existed.

Healing

The next time someone asks
you about what bit of you makes
you cringe, and what parts of
yourself you hate, trust them
enough to look at yourself and
see every flaw, and crack, and
scar, and lay yourself bare as
you let them kiss you at the
very spots that make you feel
unkissable, and remember that
healing isn't a solitary exile you
undertake till you're 'fixed' enough
to come back home, because
home is where you're fixed best.

Parachutes

"Jump," I said,
And she hesitated.

"Jump," I offered,
And she demurred.

"Jump," I asked
"But what if I fall?"

"Jump," I pleaded,
"But what if I crash?"

"Jump," I whispered,
And she dithered.

"Jump," I laughed,
And she laughed with me.

"Jump?" she asked,
And I smiled at her.

She jumped, just as I did,
And she opened her wings.

"I jumped," she said,
Wonder on her face.

"You flew," I replied,
Watching her soar away.

Lanterns

I'm going to light my heart up
and let the string binding it to me
go, and watch it float away into
the inky skies, a little ball of
love and light, leaving a trail
of embers behind, and it'll come
back to me some day, a smidgen
worse for wear, maybe a little
torn on one side, and with a few
visible repairs attempted as I cried,
but I know it will come back,
for it's truly mine, just given and
shared with all who need some
glitter in their dreary lives.

Resurgence

Wavering whispers floating over
turned soil, the loamy brown stark
against stony rock, warmth throbbing
through dirt like vitality and life,
hosting within it, corpses, large and
small; exoskeletons of dreams and
abilities lying side by side, wreathed
with shells of bodies smaller than us,
and the dead murmur up to their
skies that rest under my feet, and
I reach into the earth, muddy fingers
of the ground lacing through mine,
each inquisitive, and hesitant in its
cautious prying, and I pull out a bud,
(it leaves without much protest)
putting it to my ears, and it hums
to me a lullaby almost forgotten,
quiet dirges of longing and regret.

Instruction Manual on Missing Me

i. don't cry, you know I hated to think
I caused you pain, don't let the tears
drip off your skin, swallow them all—
salty bitter reminders of the fact that
I'm gone.

ii. don't frown, you know I hated to think
I caused you worry, don't let the lines
rest into the groove of your face, smoothen
yourself out on an ironing board—tell me
stories I'll never hear.

iii. don't call, you know I hated how your
voice sounded on the phone, narrowed from
its expanse into a tunnel of half-hearted
emotions—put it down, and change the
saved name to 'lost.'

iv. don't delete my traces off your electronic
life, watch the videos you took of me
backward—unlearn each smirk, unhinge
each expression till you've forgotten what
I tasted like.

v. don't listen to my pleas of remembrance,
I feel like I only exist in your head, I need
to know I won't billow away like smoke,
buffeted by your disregard—let me go,
I have lost my will to haunt.

Acknowledgments

I thought I was incredibly lucky to have beautiful people to mention in my first book's acknowledgments. I think, as I write this, what I'm truly, completely lucky to have is the same group of people cheering me on, and pushing me to do better. My acknowledgments this time around remain vastly unchanged, with a few notable additions. If I miss you, assume your name shines through the spaces between words.

Mamma, Papa, Sukhnidh, there's nothing without you.

Nanu, Nani, Mamu, Mami for ceaseless support, love, and inspiration.

Masi, for being.

Mahima, Mallika, Saloni, for, as usual, being constants.

Akshat, for being a lighthouse, and sometimes the anchor.

Raghav, for unrelenting hope, love, and support.

Megha, Jasmin, Annz, for a sisterhood that rallies through the strangest of times.

Devasheesh, for driving through ghost towns with me.

Shamir, because homes are people.

Taksh, for all the journeys we've known.

Ohana, for making sure no one is left behind.

Sameer, Vaishnavi, Amitoj, Mehek, because being cooped up in a hotel for forty-eight hours without sleep makes for family.

The people I've met this year, because I know we're going to have incredible adventures.

Thank you.

About the Author

Harnidh is a 22-year-old student, currently pursuing her Masters in Public Policy from St. Xavier's, Mumbai. *The Ease of Forgetting* is her second collection of poems. She feels that for all that she has tried to hold on to, it is letting go which has come easier and kinder to her.

Her first collection, *The Inability of Words* was published in 2016.

YOU MIGHT ALSO LIKE:

The First New Universe by Heidi Priebe

Bloodline by Ari Eastman

Your Soul is a River by Nikita Gill

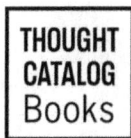

THOUGHT
CATALOG
Books

THOUGHT CATALOG

IT'S A WEBSITE.

www.thoughtcatalog.com

SOCIAL

facebook.com/thoughtcatalog
twitter.com/thoughtcatalog
tumblr.com/thoughtcatalog
instagram.com/thoughtcatalog

CORPORATE

www.thought.is

www.ingramcontent.com/pod-product-compliance
Lightning Source LLC
Chambersburg PA
CBHW031622040426

42452CB00007B/626